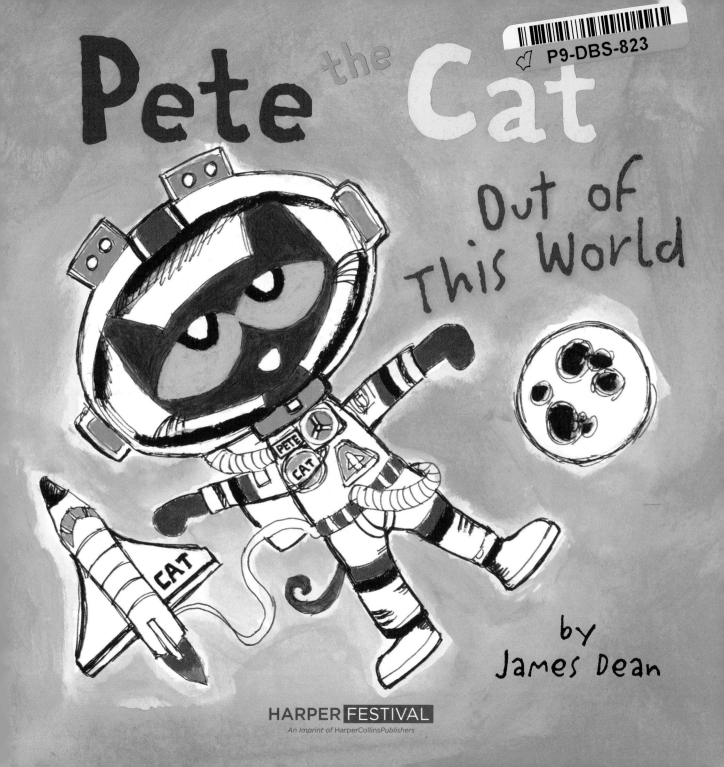

Pete the Cat

Out of This World

by James Dean

P9-DBS-823

HARPER FESTIVAL
An Imprint of HarperCollins Publishers

Harperfestival is an imprint of HarperCollins Publishers.

Pete the Cat: Out of This World
Copyright © 2017 by James Dean
All rights reserved. Printed in the United States of America.

No part of this book may be used or reproduced in any manner whatsoever without written permission
except in the case of brief quotations embodied in critical articles and reviews. For information address
HarperCollins Children's Books, a division of HarperCollins Publishers, 195 Broadway, New York, NY 10007.
www.harpercollinschildrens.com

Library of Congress Control Number: 2016961852
ISBN 978-0-06-240443-5

21 22 CWM 14 13 12 11
❖
First Edition

It's a great day. Pete the Cat is going to space camp!

Pete meets his bunk mate, Glenn. As they unpack,
there is an announcement.

"Welcome, space campers! Please head to the
classroom. Your mission begins now."

"Time to suit up," says Pete.
He and Glenn put on their uniforms and race to class.

There are so many cool things to do and super neat stuff to see.

Astronauts Tom and Kris talk about the trips they've taken. And they give a sneak peek at future space trips!

"It would be totally rad to go to space," says Pete.

The campers find out what it feels like to be an astronaut.

They go in the zero-gravity chamber.

They ride in rovers.

They even build rockets. Pete's
rocket flies very, very far.

"Way to go, Pete," shouts Glenn.

Next stop is mission control.

"We have some exciting news," says Tom. "Our next flight leaves today. We're going to the moon . . . and we have room for more."

"Pete, do you want to go?" asks Sally.
"That would be awesome," says Pete.

It's time to buckle up and settle into the space capsule.

"Five . . .

four . . .

three . . .

two . . .

one . . .

MEOW

MEOW MARS

CAT

CAT

CAT
SPACE CAMP

PETE CAT

SALLY CAT

PETE CAT

SALLY CAT

FAR OUT

ROCKET CAT

THE MOON Rocks!

Cat
Aerospace
Technology

CAT

C.A.T.

SPACE IS FAR OUT!

SPACE IS GROOVY

HARPER FESTIVAL
An Imprint of HarperCollinsPublishers
www.harpercollinschildrens.com • www.petethecatbooks.com • Illustrations copyright © 2017 by James Dean

Their ship speeds through space. They blast
past a satellite and even spot a comet.

Tom and Sally have a rockin' surprise for Pete—his guitar!

He plays a groovy interstellar song for them. Mission control listens in.

In no time at all, they arrive on the moon. They are ready to explore.

The astronauts collect rocks and map out
the moon's surface.

Pete has a very important
job to do. He straps on a
jet pack and heads toward Mars!

He takes tons of pictures.

Oh no! Pete lost track of time
and the moon is far, far away.

He has to make
it back to the ship
before it blasts off!

Phew! Pete made it
back in the nick of time.

The astronauts head home.
And there's time for a few more tunes.

Pete sure knows how to make an entrance!

Pete's trip to outer space was out of this world.
Still, he's psyched to have his feet back on solid ground.

Rocket on, Pete!